My Grandpa's full name

Date of birth

Place of birth

My Grandpa's mother's full name

Date of birth

Place of birth

My Grandpa's father's full name

Date of birth

Place of birth

Grandpa, your life is a gift.

You hold within you a story that only you can share. Use these pages to fill with your one-of-a-kind memories— whether it's a special moment from your childhood, information about your heritage, an unforgettable adventure, or a piece of advice to share. Speak from the heart, in your own words—it doesn't need to be formal or complex. Because when you are finished, you will create a gift that will be loved for generations.

GENERATIONS

What are some stories about your own grandparents? Where were they born? Do you remember what they looked like? What were their personalities like?

Family faces are magic mirrors. Looking at people who belong to us, we see the past, present, and future.

Gail Lumet Buckley

Sentimental
KEEPSAKES

What are some family heirlooms or mementos you've
kept, and why are they special to you?

_____

_____

_____

_____

_____

_____

_____

_____

_____

_____

_____

_____

Family
RELATIONSHIPS

What was your relationship like with your parents?

_____

_____

_____

_____

_____

_____

_____

_____

_____

_____

_____

_____

_____

_____

Did you have any special relationships with any other family members?

_____

_____

_____

_____

_____

_____

_____

_____

_____

_____

_____

_____

Being
A KID

What do you miss most about being a kid? It could be a specific activity or perhaps a feeling you miss.

_____

_____

_____

_____

_____

_____

_____

_____

_____

_____

_____

_____

Childhood
lasts all
through life.

Gaston Bachelard

JOYS OF
childhood

Places you liked to play growing up:

_____

_____

_____

_____

_____

_____

_____

Favorite family meals or recipes:

_____

_____

_____

_____

_____

_____

School subjects that you loved:

First MEMORIES

What is your earliest memory?

_____

_____

_____

_____

When you were little, how would you get to school?

_____

_____

_____

As a child, you were afraid of:

_____

_____

_____

_____

_____

Your favorite toys were:

_____

_____

_____

You've always had a natural talent for:

_____

_____

_____

_____

Some of the chores you had growing up were:

_____

_____

_____

_____

_____

_____

SIBLINGS & *friendships*

What was your relationship like with your siblings, and what stories do you remember about them? You can also describe great childhood friends and the adventures you had with them.

_____

_____

_____

_____

_____

_____

_____

_____

_____

_____

_____

_____

_____

_____

_____

_____

Truly there is
nothing in the world
so blessed or so sweet
as the heritage
of children.

Margaret Oliphant

CHILDHOOD
home

What was your home like growing up? Include details like the neighborhood, who lived with you, what your room was like, and how and where your family spent time together.

_____

_____

_____

_____

_____

_____

_____

_____

_____

_____

_____

_____

Music,
MOVIES & BOOKS

Favorite childhood books:

_____

_____

_____

_____

Favorite childhood movies:

_____

_____

_____

_____

Favorite childhood music:

_____

_____

_____

_____

Favorite childhood games or sports:

_____

_____

_____

_____

_____

_____

Favorite childhood hobbies, interests, or collections:

_____

_____

_____

_____

_____

_____

_____

TIME
Travel

If you could go back in time to relive any moment in your life, what would it be? And why?

_____

_____

_____

_____

_____

_____

_____

_____

_____

_____

_____

_____

_____

...history
isn't just the past.
It's alive in us.

Natalie Portman

COSTS OF
living

How much did these cost when you were growing up?

A gallon of milk:

_____

_____

_____

_____

_____

A movie ticket:

_____

_____

_____

_____

_____

_____

_____

A new car:

_____

_____

Your first paying job was:

_____

_____

_____

How old you were when you started:

_____

_____

_____

You were paid this much:

_____

_____

_____

Being a
FATHER

What was it like to become a father?

_____

_____

_____

_____

_____

_____

What are some of your very first memories of your own children?

_____

_____

_____

_____

_____

_____

_____

The love
we give away is
the only love
we keep.

Elbert Hubbard

Clever INVENTIONS

Things that have been created after you had children that you wish you had:

_____

_____

_____

_____

_____

_____

_____

_____

_____

_____

_____

_____

_____

HOLIDAY
Traditions

What was your favorite holiday to celebrate when your children were growing up? What were some holiday traditions that you had?

_____

_____

_____

_____

_____

_____

_____

_____

_____

_____

_____

_____

_____

_____

Grandparents
are a family's greatest
treasure, the founders
of a loving legacy...

Unknown

LITTLE
rascals

List times when your own children did something that drove you crazy or tested family rules:

_____

_____

_____

_____

_____

_____

_____

_____

_____

_____

_____

_____

_____

SIGNS OF *affection*

How do you show your love to your children or grandchildren? Do you shower them with gifts? Praise their successes? Maybe you gently encourage them to do their best or have a special tradition just between you. Share them here:

_____

_____

_____

_____

_____

_____

_____

_____

_____

_____

_____

_____

By giving children
lots of affection, you can
help fill them with love
and acceptance
of themselves...

Wayne Dyer

WORDS TO
remember

Things you've often said to your children or grandchildren:

_____

_____

_____

_____

_____

_____

_____

_____

_____

_____

_____

_____

_____

Things your children or grandchildren have said that you'll never forget:

_____

_____

_____

_____

_____

_____

_____

_____

_____

_____

_____

_____

_____

Life MOTTO

What is your favorite quote or saying? Or maybe you have several? Share them here and describe what they mean to you.

_____

_____

_____

_____

_____

_____

_____

_____

_____

_____

_____

_____

_____

Impressive
CHILDREN

In what ways do your children or grandchildren make you proud?

_____

_____

_____

_____

_____

_____

_____

_____

_____

_____

_____

_____

_____

...when I embrace
my grandfather I
experience a sense of
richness as though I am
a note in the heartbeats
of the very universe.

Tayeb Salih

YOUR

One of your favorite colors is:

_____

_____

Most days, you're wearing:

_____

_____

_____

Your favorite dessert is:

_____

_____

_____

A smell that makes you stop every time is:

_____

_____

_____

You love playing this game:

_____

_____

_____

A book that has stuck with you is:

_____

_____

_____

Music you love to listen to is:

_____

_____

Your favorite movie of all time is:

_____

_____

You're happiest when you are:

_____

_____

BEING A

What was it like to become a grandfather? How has it affected your relationship with your own children?

_____

_____

_____

_____

_____

_____

_____

_____

_____

_____

_____

_____

_____

_____

Fortunate
are the people
whose roots
are deep.

Agnes E. Meyer

YOUR BEST

qualities

What are some things people often compliment you on?

_____

_____

_____

_____

_____

_____

Which one means the most to you and why?

_____

_____

_____

_____

_____

_____

Personality
TRAITS

What about you has stayed the same throughout your life?
What's changed?

_____

_____

_____

_____

_____

_____

_____

_____

_____

_____

_____

_____

_____

_____

[Kids] don't
remember what
you try to teach them.
They remember
what you are.

Jim Henson

World
EVENTS

What major events have you witnessed in your life? Where were you and how did they affect you?

_____

_____

_____

_____

_____

_____

_____

_____

_____

_____

_____

_____

_____

LIFE
lessons

What have been some of the hardest challenges for you in life? How have they affected you? What did you learn or gain from them?

_____

_____

_____

_____

_____

_____

_____

_____

_____

_____

_____

_____

_____

_____

Learning is
ever young,
even in old age.

Aeschylus

Three THINGS

3 things you're proud of:

_____

_____

_____

_____

_____

_____

3 things you're passionate about:

_____

_____

_____

_____

_____

_____

3 things you've lost:

_____

_____

_____

_____

_____

_____

3 things you look forward to:

_____

_____

_____

_____

_____

_____

FUTURE
dreams

What are some things you have yet to do and would like to accomplish in your lifetime?

_____

_____

_____

_____

_____

_____

_____

_____

_____

_____

_____

_____

While we try
to teach our children
all about life, our
children teach us what
life is all about.

Angela Schwindt

Role MODELS

Who did you look up to as a child?

_____

_____

_____

Why?

_____

_____

_____

_____

_____

_____

_____

_____

_____

Who do you look up to now?

_____

_____

_____

Why?

_____

_____

_____

_____

_____

_____

_____

_____

_____

_____

Sound
ADVICE

If you could pass along one piece of advice, what would you say?

_____

_____

_____

_____

_____

_____

_____

_____

_____

_____

_____

_____

_____

A loving
heart is the
truest wisdom.

Charles Dickens

GRANDFATHER
joys

What's the best (or most fun) thing about being a grandfather?

_____

_____

_____

_____

_____

_____

_____

_____

_____

_____

_____

_____

_____

_____

What are some things you love about your grandchildren?

_____

_____

_____

_____

_____

_____

_____

_____

_____

_____

_____

_____

_____

A LASTING

What wishes do you have for your children and grandchildren?

_____

_____

_____

_____

_____

_____

_____

_____

_____

_____

_____

_____

_____

When you look
at your life, the
greatest happinesses
are family
happinesses.

Joyce Brothers

COMPENDIUM.
live inspired

Written by: Miriam Hathaway
Designed by: Steve Potter
Edited by: Amelia Riedler and Bailey Vega

ISBN: 978-1-970147-83-4

1st printing. Printed in China with soy inks on FSC®-Mix certified paper.

Create meaningful moments with gifts that inspire.

CONNECT WITH US
live-inspired.com | sayhello@compendiuminc.com

  @compendiumliveinspired
#compendiumliveinspired